C000318515

HAMSTERS

CO-020

A Satin Hamster. The satinized fur is now being bred in many of the color varieties of hamsters, including the longhaired or angora hamsters. Photo by Michael Gilroy.

A pair of Cream Hamsters. Photo by Michael Gilroy.

HAMSTERS

COMPLETELY ILLUSTRATED IN FULL COLOR

Mervin F. Roberts

The Dominant Spot is one of the many varieties developed from the pied mutation in hamsters. Photo by Michael Gilroy.

Distributed in the UNITED STATES by T.F.H. Publications, Inc., 211 West Sylvania Avenue, Neptune City, NJ 07753; in CANADA to the Pet Trade by H & L Pet Supplies Inc., 27 Kingston Crescent, Kitchener, Ontario N2B 2T6; Rolf C. Hagen Ltd., 3225 Sartelon Street, Montreal 382 Quebec; in CANADA to the Book Trade by Macmillan of Canada (A Division of Canada Publishing Corporation), 164 Commander Boulevard, Agincourt, Ontario M1S 3C7; in ENGLAND by T.F.H. Publications Limited, 4 Kier Park, Ascot, Berkshire SL5 7DS; in AUSTRALIA AND THE SOUTH PACIFIC by T.F.H. (Australia) Pty. Ltd., Box 149, Brookvale 2100 N.S.W., Australia; in NEW ZEALAND by Ross Haines & Son, Ltd., 18 Monmouth Street, Grey Lynn, Auckland 2 New Zealand; in SINGAPORE AND MALAYSIA by MPH Distributors (S) Pte., Ltd., 601 Sims Drive, #03/07/21, Singapore 1438; in the PHILIPPINES by Bio-Research, 5 Lippay Street, San Lorenzo Village, Makati Rizal; in SOUTH AFRICA by Multipet Pty. Ltd., 30 Turners Avenue, Durban 4001. Published by T.F.H. Publications Inc. Manufactured in the United States of America by T.F.H. Publications, Inc.

Contents

Hamsters In General

Many books about pets start with an apology of some sort. Your parakeet (they say) is really a budgerigar. A guinea pig is not a pig from Guinea but a cavy. A pet chameleon is actually an anole. An alligator is probably a caiman. And don't be surprised, you're told, if some rabbits are really hares.

But here is a book about a hamster, which is exactly and precisely a hamster. It has a perfectly legitimate Latin name—*Mesocricetus auratus*—but even the scientists just call it a hamster.

Originally—before selective breeding produced a greater variety in color and hair length—all pet hamsters were roughly golden in color. A majority still are, with soft, short golden-red fur over their backs and sides and darker marks—"flashes"—on their foreheads and cheeks, and with bellies bluish-gray to white.

The hamster's skin is very loose on its body (it can be pulled over an inch from almost every part of the body). Eyes are bright and bold and curious, but eyesight is not keen. The feet are good at grasping. The tail is merely a stump, about one-quarter of an inch long; in fact a male of the longhaired variety generally has his tail completely hidden by his long hair.

Below: *The Syrian hamster is commonly called the golden hamster. Photo by P. Parslow.*

An unusual feature of hamsters, setting them apart from most other animals, is the cheek pouch, which is used for gathering food and litter for nests and for preparing the nest litter. The pouches extend from the cheeks to the shoulder and can hold food approximately equal to one-half of the animal's volume. The inside is a soft tissue which slightly moistens the material being stored. The pouches do not really stand out except when they are full and the animal is viewed from above.

Above: *Another species of hamster that can be considered as a good pet is the dwarf hamster or small desert hamster. Its coat color and markings are quite distinct from the golden hamster. Photo by Michael Gilroy.*

The story of the golden hamster as a pet began in 1930, when Professor I. Aharoni of the Department of Zoology of Hebrew University, Jerusalem, acquired an adult female and her litter of twelve babies near Aleppo, Syria. A few months afterward, he gave one male and two

Above: *One can spend much time just watching the entertaining behavior of a pet hamster.*

females of the wild litter to the university, and there Dr. Ben-Menahem first bred them. This trio is believed to be the source of every living hamster today. Some of the young were sent to England in 1931, and from there a few were shipped to the United States Public Health Service Research at Carville, Louisiana, where they were used for medical research.

It was the research scientists who first noticed that hamsters made fine pets, and it was probably from the stock at Carville that hamsters became available to the public. By now there are certainly more hamsters in captivity than there are in all the hamster burrows in Syria.

WHY HAVE A HAMSTER AS A PET?

Today there are millions of hamsters giving affection and amusement to their owners. The fact that they are easy to care for, gentle, attractive and very entertaining makes them especially suitable as pets in small quarters.

Hamsters are small animals, which means that they can be comfortable in relatively small quarters—which in turn means that people who are beginning with hamsters don't have to make a large cash outlay for the hamsters' housing. Pet shops sell a wide variety of good but inexpensive hamster accommodations.

A hamster is a cuddly, hand-holdable pet. It is larger than a mouse and has a prettier face. And it doesn't have the musky odor of a male mouse.

Hamsters are amusing animals. They sit up, stand on their hind legs, sit like bears and climb and grasp practically anything they can get their "hands" on. They can grasp with their hind feet as well, and they enjoy doing acrobatic tricks.

Hamsters are gentle, clean, odorless and practically mute. They won't utter annoying noises.

While most pets need daily care, hamsters can be left alone over a weekend if necessary, because they hoard food and don't drink much.

Hamsters' hoarding habit

Above. *Note the difference in the size and dorsal coat marking between a dwarf hamster and a golden hamster variety. Photo by Michael Gilroy.*

Below: Two young dwarf hamsters. It is not surprising that breeders will develop new varieties by selective breeding. Photo by Michael Gilroy.

makes them especially interesting to watch. (The name hamster, incidentally, comes from the German *hamstern,* meaning "to hoard.") You will be fascinated as you watch a hamster stuff food into its enormous cheek pouches and then take it out and hide it "for a rainy day."

Hamsters are handsome little animals, and they come in several colors and textures; they also come in short-haired and longhaired forms.

Hamsters are hardy and easy to breed. And talk about speedy! They are unique in their ability to reproduce themselves only sixteen days after mating. So, if you want a family of them, or if you're thinking of unusual presents for your friends and relatives, you need not wait long.

Their life span is about 1000 days maximum, so if you get tired of keeping hamsters, just stop breeding them and in less than three years you will be free. And a bit lonely.

They enjoy being hand-fed, played with and fondled. Their fur is soft and pleasant to

Below: *Through selective breeding of Syrian hamsters several varieties that are quite different from the wild type have been developed. Photo by Michael Gilroy.*

Above: *Note the dissimilar facial markings of these young hamsters that also have longer fur than the common pet hamster. Photo by Michael Gilroy.*

Right: *In the wild golden hamsters leave their burrows to feed outside where they often become prey of larger animals. Feeding at night and storing the food in cheek pouches increase their chances for survival.*

touch. If one escapes, it will probably be happy to return to its cage.

Grooming is a cinch. Their teeth and nails generally wear down as they grow and need no attention. There's no reason to bathe a hamster (isn't that a relief!); it will groom itself clean as long as it's healthy. Even the coat of the longhaired variety needs only an occasional gentle brushing.

How To Choose A Hamster

A few minutes of observation of hamsters in a pet shop will probably convince you that it would be fun to own one. The next step is to choose the one for you.

Age

It is best to get your hamster just a few weeks after it has been weaned away from its mother—at about five weeks of age. Luckily, however, the hamster is so gentle and so easily tamed that even a year-old anaimal can be trained without too much difficulty. But there's another good reason for choosing a baby, if you're being really practical.

Below: *A young female hamster of a special variety. She has satin-like fur and is a carrier of the banded trait of coat pattern. Photo by Michael Gilroy.*

Aquariums used as hamster homes have the advantage of keeping drafts off the hamsters and of course provide good visibility and are completely non-chewable. This aquarium unit has been safely locked under a screen cover. Photo courtesy Penn-Plax Plastics.

Since hamsters live only about a thousand days and cost as little as they do, you can figure that a year-old hamster has already lived out a chunk of your investment. On the other hand, a hamster younger than thirty days is too young to move, too young to play with and too young to have good control of its emotions or its locomotion. Baby hamsters have poor vision, and those under thirty days will have a great deal of trouble seeing things—the edge of a table, for instance. While older hamsters will come to the edge of a table and stop, the baby will often go right over the edge and topple to the floor. This is dangerous because, unlike mice, hamsters don't seem to be able to flip about in the air and fall lightly on their feet.

Sex

Your hamster can be of either sex, since both males and females make good pets. A pair could make thousands of good pets. A word of warning, though: don't buy a pair unless you know in advance what you are going to do with the babies. Pet shops can probably obtain exactly what the market calls for, when there is a demand, more readily from commercial breeders than from individuals such as you. Don't plan to make your pets pay for themselves.

Male hamsters often seem to be more even-tempered and friendly than females; this may be due to the female's sensitivity during pregnancy and her negative reaction to having her newborn pup molested.

Among the longhairs the male seems to have the *slightly* longer coat.

Mature males have one or two black dots over their hips under the fur. Each is about as large as the hamster's eye and about two or three times the thickness of the skin. These marks are quite normal. They are called dimorphic pigment spots and are much like "beauty marks" in humans. Some perfectly healthy hamsters will lick these spots in warm weather. Large lumps, boils, abscesses and pimples are another matter, of course.

Below: *Two superb varieties of Syrian hamsters, a fawn female on the left and a black-eyed female on the right. They are also shorthaired hamsters. Photo by Michael Gilroy.*

Appearance

The size of your pet when you buy it is primarily dependent on its age. However, it should weigh fifty four grams (about an ounce and a half) or more. A hamster smaller than that will have the same trouble as a very young one. The shape and general appearance of the hamster you choose is very important. Lumps, bumps, discoloration, loose hair, wet bottom or tail, stuffed or running nose, running eyes, blood anywhere and bad disposition are all symptoms which should stop you from making a purchase. Don't buy anything but a perfectly healthy pet! Then you can look forward to keeping it free from disease

Above: *A true albino hamster will have the characteristic pink eyes.*

Below: *The special feature of this female cream hamster is her beautiful fur, silky and soft like satin. Photo by Michael Gilroy.*

Above: *This longhaired albino hamster will require some grooming in order to keep the coat in good condition. Photo by Brian Seed.*

for the next thousand days or so. The signs of good health are soft, silken fur, plump body, a general feeling of solidity to the body, prominent bright eyes and an alert inquisitiveness.

A tiny nick or hole on a hamster's ear may be a breeder's mark, or it may be the result of a bite from a cagemate. It is not a disease, and unless you plan to exhibit your pet in a competitive show you can ignore it.

The hamster you choose should have a gentle disposition. If it is nasty and doesn't allow you to pick it up, don't buy it.

Varieties

Hamsters today are bred in several different colors. Among the common colors are the albino, which is white with pink eyes; the pied, harlequin or panda, which are all spotted brown or beige on white with dark eyes; and a cream or beige or fawn variety with brown or ruby eyes. This latter type has several names—which are given by individual breeders but have not yet been established by common use.

Longhaired hamsters tend to cost more than shorthairs. They tend to be a bit less prolific.

Pink-eyed hamsters may have poorer vision than dark-eyed varieties. *Some* pink-eyed hamsters are known to be blind or nearly blind, but since most white hamsters are not pink-eyed but rather ruby-eyed, the problem is not as prevalent as one might suppose.

Of all of them the most hardy is the ordinary golden (or "Syrian") variety.

Below: *The longhaired coat in hamsters has been bred in a variety of colors, the gray shown here. Photo by Michael Gilroy.*

Price

Be prepared to pay a respectableprice for your pet. A hamster that costs *too* little is not really a bargain.

Your hamster should come from a reputable local pet shop. Operators of such shops know their sources of supply, so they sell only healthy animals. A variety/discount store is the worst place to buy a hamster. The help is usually uninformed, the management is usually uninterested, and the livestock usually is of uncertain quality.

HAMSTER BEHAVIOR

Your pet hamster wants to explore, to play, to hide, to hoard food, to keep clean with fresh bedding and to be handled gently. Once you understand your hamster's habits, training will be easy, and you'll have a pet you can really enjoy.

First of all, hamsters like privacy—privacy from humans and also privacy from *all* other animals and *most* other hamsters. A few young specimens of the same sex do well together, but an adult female will sometimes kill a male who is introduced into her cage when she is not receptive. If you plan to keep several hamsters together in one cage, provide plenty of room, with separate nest boxes or other hiding places. Keep the sexes separate, and watch the hamsters for signs of fighting. If they do fight, separate them immediately.

Hamsters like to crawl into and explore cave-like articles, perhaps because those articles provide them with a sense of security. Pet shops carry numerous safe products, such as the two shown here, to satisfy hamsters' "holing-up" instincts. Photos courtesy Penn-Plax Plastics.

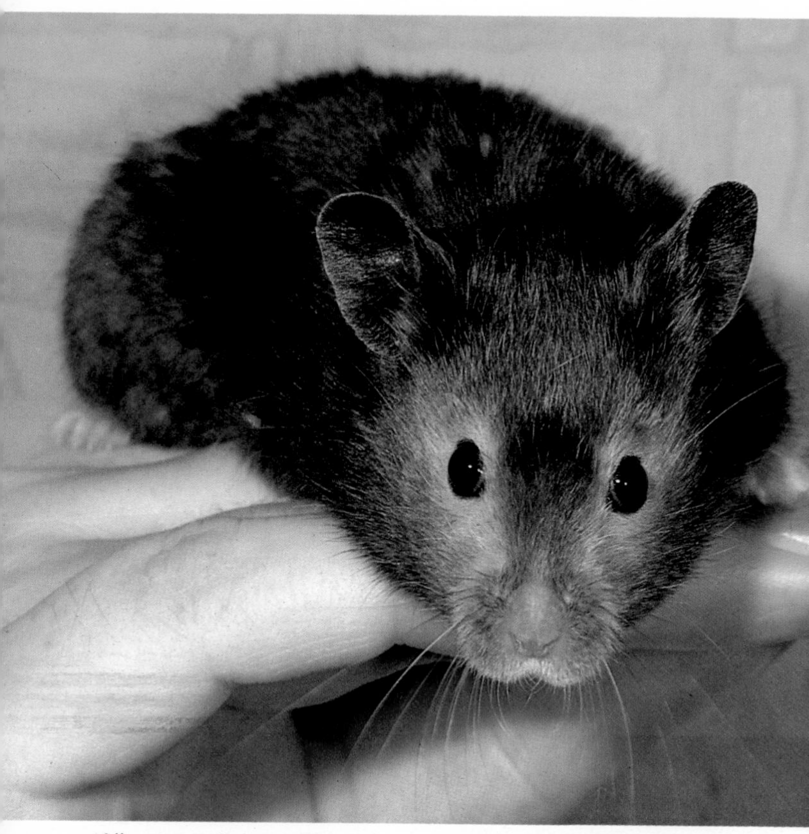

Allow your hamster to get used to you before you pick it up. As you and your pet become more accustomed to one another, you may find that it is perfectly all right to reach into the cage, but don't do it the first day. When you pick up your hamster, lift his body gently. Don't grasp him by the skin or tail or leg or around the neck. Let it climb into your hand.

Hamsters are nocturnal animals, sleeping during the day. They do not like sunlight or any bright light. However, if you want to play with your hamster during the day it will not object if you awaken it gently and keep it out of the bright light until it is thoroughly awake. Don't breathe heavily or blow on your hamster. A warning sign is when your hamster's ears are curled or laid back. This

Above: *A fully tamed hamster will welcome being handled by you. Constant handling re-enforces taming. Photo by Burkhard Kahl.*

Right: *It will be best to resist handling the newly born or very young hamsters. Except in very rare cases the female hamster will feed and groom her young regularly. Photo by John Hall.*

often happens when you first waken it or when you disturb a mother hamster. Be patient, and soon the ears will open out and stand erect. Then you can feel reasonably sure that your pet isn't mad at you. Hamsters are naturally friendly with humans, and you will get along well by acting thoughtful and humane.

Baby hamsters are not "housebroken." They soil the cage anywhere, but since they are clean animals, by the time they are about two months old their good habits will be well established.

Hamsters have a strong feeling about what is theirs. This applies to their hoards, their homes and their babies. A pet hamster might nip its owner's hand if the hand is thrust into the hamster's nest or even into its cage, but the same animal will be perfectly safe and tame and friendly if it is outside the cage.

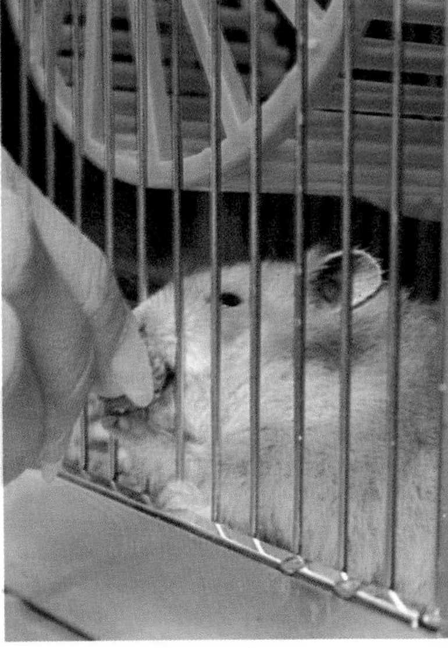

Above: *Giving your pet a tasty morsel now and then is harmless. However, be selective of the type of food you offer. Photo by Dr. Herbert R. Axelrod.*

Sometimes females have a stronger desire to accumulate and hoard food and nesting materials than males. Male hamsters live alone and do not join in any family affairs. The male may, in fact, destroy the young, or he may be destroyed himself by the female if he ventures near the babies.

This is extremely important: A pregnant female or a new mother should be left strictly alone until the babies' eyes are open—when they are about 16 days old. Here's why:

The hamster's eyesight is not especially good, but its senses of hearing and smell are acute; in fact, like other rodents, hamsters are very

Exercise wheels for hamsters come in a number of different styles and colors and materials. The colorful exercise wheel shown and its stand, for example, are made of plastic. Photo courtesy Penn-Plax Plastics.

smell-oriented. In a non-scientific yet practical sense their "brain" is in their nose. Your strongly non-hamster odor interferes with the familiar smell of the litter and greatly disorients the mother. Many mothers have killed or deserted their litters because the pet owner didn't know this or didn't have the patience and strength of character to leave the hamsters alone at this time. Of course the first few days are the most crucial, and as time goes on the mother becomes more tolerant.

Hamsters replace their fur about every three months. As they grow old there is a tendency for less hair to appear on the ears, until at last the ears appear quite shiny.

Hamsters hibernate, especially if the air is both moist and cold. If you keep your pet in a cage out of doors, provide a draft-free sleeping area which it can arrange to suit itself during its period of hibernation.

There is a possibility that the life span of the hamster is connected with the amount of hibernation. A hamster that hibernates two months a year may live longer than the 1000 days usually allotted. This is a field that would benefit from study by serious pet keepers.

Housing

In general, buy, don't build. The thrill of personal accomplishment is wonderful indeed, but unfortunately anything you can build can be bought for less, and it might very well be better. You may probably build no more than a handful of hamster cages in your lifetime, but a cage manufacturer produces thousands and probably has worked out bugs you never thought of.

For large-scale breeding try stainless steel or plastic boxes with ⅜ inch wire mesh covers. For a small scale home hobby, consider an aquarium, or a birdcage, or a cage especially for small rodents available at your pet shop.

The pink fabric hanging from the cage in the form of an inverted umbrella prevents scattering of cage contents during transport.

Cupping the hands around your pet hamster gives it a sense of security that is reminiscent of close quarters in a burrow. Illustration by Richard Crammer.

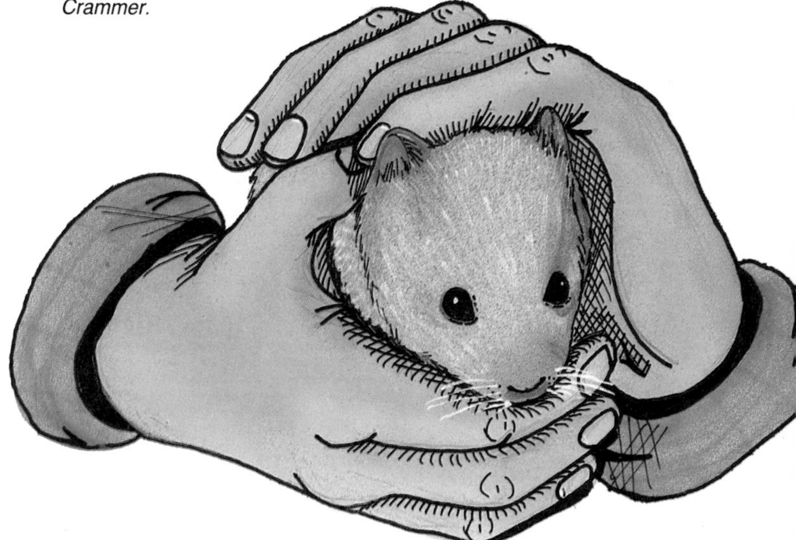

Avoid a cage having a wooden bottom. The wood will soak up the urine and will always be damp and smelly. Plastic, glass or stainless steel are all good cagebottom materials. Another reason for not recommending wood as a cage material is that it can be gnawed. If the wood is splintery and sharp it can hurt the hamster's mouth or cheek pouches. If it is thin, you may have an escape to contend with.

Try for something strong and simple. Remember there must be an access for water. A water dish will not work, as your hamster will quickly and deliberately fill it with bedding or feces. Hamsters are desert animals—they drink drops of dew hanging from plants, but standing water is foreign to their way of life. Don't try to change them. Remember that a hamster is a granivorous desert rodent—what little water it needs should be clean, fresh and dew-like. The water access is best handled with a bottle, rubber stopper and glass tube—from above.

The cover should latch. Not gadgety—but simple and strong and easy to lock. As escape artists, hamsters are rivaled only by snakes, monkeys and parrots.

The cover might well provide ventilation. If the cover is coarsely screened it will also be attractive to the hamster for exercise. The hamster will climb about, upside down, for hours, every night. The wire will also get its share of gnawing, which is nothing more than teeth-sharpening and release of nervous tension.

They may not look very athletic, but hamsters are fairly adept at climbing and even (as can be seen here) at swinging themselves "hand over hand" along the bars of their cage. ➤

ACCESSORIES

An exercise wheel is great if you can find room for it and don't mind the squeaking of the bearings all through the night. Never during the day—only at night! There may be a silent exercise wheel—find it if you can. Hamsters *do* need to exercise; if they don't, they are subject to paralysis.

A series of normal attitudes a hamster can display inside or outside the cage. Illustration by John R. Quinn.

A long-haired hamster using an exercise wheel to good advantage. Such wheels are inexpensive, and considering the amount of fun they provide for both hamsters and their owners, they're a very good investment. Photo by Mervin F. Roberts.

BEDDING

Weaned hamsters develop toilet habits with a little help from you. The urine is the problem, since the droppings tend to dry out quickly, and dry droppings are virtually odorless. Here is where you can help.

Provide plenty of bedding which your hamster can move around the cage. It will hide food in certain areas, build its nest elsewhere and sweep clean the spot where it leaves its liquid wastes. As the wastes evaporate, you can scrape up the remainder and then blot up the last traces with a small wad of bedding which should then be thrown away.

Clean the cage often enough to keep the urine spot localized. If the *entire* cage is dirty or damp, the animal will have no cause to choose a particular spot to wet. How often? Once every week or two is good point. If you clean the cage too frequently, you will waste food and disturb the hamster's sense of security by ruining the nest and the hoard.

Above: *Wood chips are sold in pet shops for bedding of small mammals like hamsters, gerbils, guinea pigs, mice, and others. Photo by Michael Gilroy.*

Below: *Shredded paper helps keep the wood chip bedding dry by absorbing urine in this holding bin with young hamsters and parent. Photo by Brian Seed.*

Remember to clean the cage of a female *while* she is being mated. She will be too busy to be bothered by your housecleaning. This technique will permit her to establish a nursery in anticipation of delivering a litter two weeks hence. Don't touch her cage contents again until the young are weaned. Since this whole process will take a month or so, it will be a good idea to provide extra bedding in this instance.

Bedding can be nearly anything which is not poisonous, overly aromatic, sharp or entangling. Paper confetti, wood chips, sawdust, shavings, mowed hay, chopped hay, cotton waste, have all been used successfully. Mr. Richard Smith of Stonehill Farms, Groton, Connecticut buys aspen wood shavings, even though he could get for free all the hay or sawdust he could possibly use. Aspen, a type of poplar, is a soft wood—it is not aromatic like cedar, nor is it full of pitch like some of the pines. Two heaping handfuls provide a two-week supply for an adult and several youngsters together in a cage.

A longhaired hamster might

Below: *Wood shavings clinging to the fur of this cinnamon hamster can be easily brushed off to avoid tangles, especially in longhaired varieties. Photo by Michael Gilroy.*

Above: *Anything resembling a burrow will be occupied by a hamster. Photo by M. Gilroy.*

get its hair tangled in the wood shavings, but with a dry toothbrush you can eliminate the tangles before they become a problem.

One accessory for the cage is a plastic, glass or metal scoop. It should be a little larger than your largest hamster. Use it to transfer a female to the cage of the male for breeding. There are two good reasons for this. First, there is less chance of your being bitten. Remember, your hand is hamster size and it is invading another hamster's castle. Second, a female should smell like a female; she should not smell like your hand when she is introduced to the male. Perhaps your scoop can be a kitchen utensil, the kind some cooks use for dipping into flour or sugar. Another way to create a handy scoop is by cutting off the bottom and part of one side of a plastic bottle.

When you clean cages, don't use insect sprays or dusts since some may be dangerous to your animals, and if you provide 100% fresh clean bedding, the insects and insect eggs will be kept

Above: *Adequate ventilation is crucial when keeping hamsters in an aquarium or glass tank. Photo by Dr. Herbert R. Axelrod.*

Below: *Children,in particular, think that a HABITRAIL unit will keep a hamster happy. Photo by Dr. Herbert R. Axelrod.*

under control or entirely eliminated without the need for insecticides. This is not really a problem if you keep fewer than a hundred animals and don't introduce new stock directly "off-the-street."

If you expect to introduce additional hamsters to your stock, one or two cages should be kept empty and apart—in another room if possible—as quarantine for new or sick animals.

Living World has introduced onto the pet market a popular unit they call "HABITRAIL." This is a well-conceived and well-manufactured expandable home, playground, gymnasium and easy-to-clean unit which is difficult to describe. You have to see it.

The cage should have a secluded area for sleeping and hoarding, and enough space for "toilet facilities" away from the sleeping and hoarding areas. It should have water, draft-free ventilation, and dry, warm cage litter. Wood shavings are best, but torn up newspaper can also be used. Keep the cage away from sunlight or any bright, glaring light. An average temperature of 68 F. is fine.

Unhappy hamsters are usually those that are crowded, not permitted seclusion, deprived of a place to hoard food, or abused by their cagemates. However, even if your hamster has a comforable home, he may try to escape. This is only the result of his natural curiosity.

Above: *Ladders for small mammals are standard accessories offered by pet shops. Photo by Michael Gilroy.*

Below: *Another common equipment for your hamster cage is the revolving wheel. Photo by Michael Gilroy.*

Above: *Regardless of how tame your house cat is, be sure your hamsters are safe from it. To a cat your pet is not any different from a mouse or a rat. The cage must be securely covered. Illustration by John R. Quinn.*

ESCAPES AND CAPTURES

The hamster spends a great deal of his time plotting and figuring out ways to escape. He gnaws, digs, scratches, pushes and gnaws some more. And he waits. But at least once he will find his way out, and that's that.

Escapes are a problem several ways. New Mexico has a climate like Syria—you have no business establishing, even by accident, an exotic rodent where he might take over from resident species. Another problem is that an escaped hamster might pick up parasites, ticks, fleas or disease and then when you capture him and put him back in the colony, you have introduced an open Pandora's box. Still another is the possibility of loss to a predator; to a dog, a cat or a rat a hamster is fair and likely game. Unfortunately, unlike a squirrel or hare, a hamster can't run fast enough to escape them.

The chances of finding a hamster under the ottoman, in the broom closet, in the piano or television set is comparable to those of finding the proverbial needle in the haystack. You won't find him by searching, but you can recapture him easily enough. All you need is a carrot, a deep pail with smooth sides (or a smooth metal wastebasket) and a few bricks or blocks of wood. Another hamster (preferably a female if the escapee is a male) will help. So will some of the wood shavings and nest material taken from the hamster cage. This is what you do: First cover all toilets and aquariums, drain the bathtubs and sinks, and put out the cat. Actually, "put out the cat" should be the *first* thing you do. Before you go to bed, set the pail on the floor. Pile the bricks or blocks to form an outside stairway. Rub the carrot up the "steps" and drop it into the pail. Place the wood shavings with the carrot. Put the other caged hamster, if you have one, on the floor alongside the pail. Then go to sleep. In the morning the escaped hamster will be in with the shavings; it happens every time.

It's advisable that the female hamster, if you are using her as bait, be in a small separate cage within the trap. It's for *his* protection; if she's not in a receptive mood she just might kill the poor thing after he falls in.

Hamsters are also fond of pipes, tubes, conduits, tunnels and similar long, dark spaces. You can take advantage of this knowledge by trying a live trap—there are many in the marketplace. Most are tunnel-shaped with one or two doors at the ends and a treadle in the center. They work. Bait the treadle with something sticky—like peanut butter, with some grain pressed into it.

Below: *This is a standard show and carrying cage made in Great Britain. Being small, it is not intended for housing hamsters. Photo by M. Gilroy.*

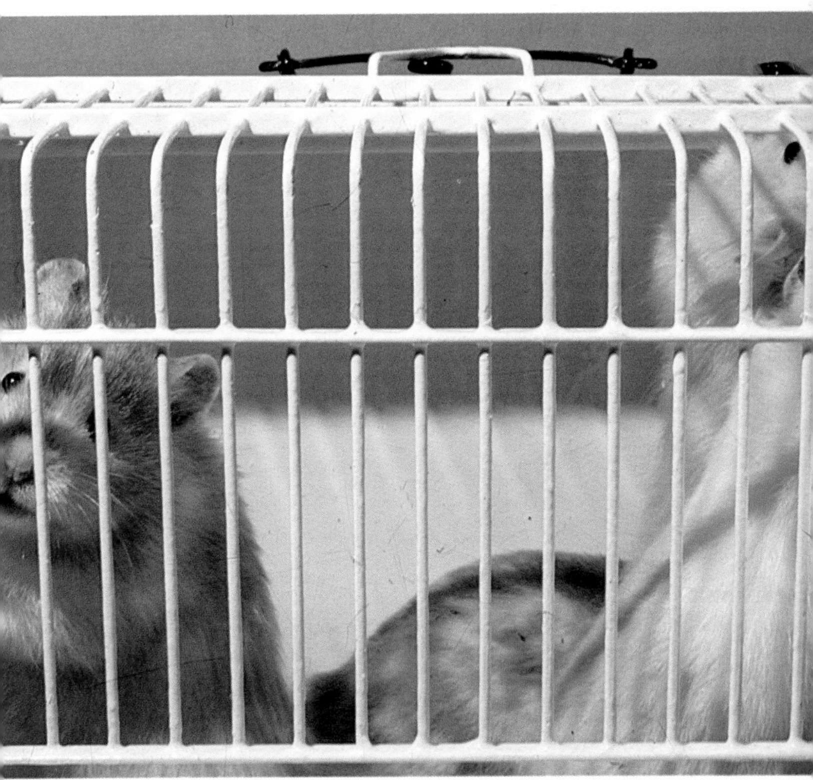

SOME POISONOUS PLANTS.

If you have any mice in the house and they get trapped with the hamster, he will probably kill them. But a rat will almost surely kill the hamster, so don't leave the "trap" any longer than necessary if there are any rats around.

Even though escape is almost inevitable, you can try to prevent it. Your hamster is not quite quicksilver, but he can get through any opening as large as his head. He's a tiny animal, and rather than risk a loss you should make sure the cage is as strong and tight as possible, with an outside latch of some sort.

Feeding

Hamsters are gnawing animals. They are therefore slow eaters, eaters of seeds, nuts and hard foods. Although they do enjoy soft foods, they are designed and equipped to consume hard materials which are slowly chewed and slowly digested. Because of this hamsters are constant nibblers. This also helps to explain the value of the hoarding instinct and the cheek pouches; hamsters just naturally want to forage for food and carry it in their pouches to a hiding place to eat at leisure. If hamsters' food were of a soft, quick-spoiling nature this would not be possible—and soft, quick-spoiling foods are also extremely difficult to *remove* from the pouch; remaining stuck there, they are the source of various health problems.

Whether you feed your pet once a day at a specified time, or you simply replenish the stock for his hoard when it runs low, it is he who will decide when to eat and what to eat. You may sometimes notice that your hamster is eating when he looks half asleep—with his eyes closed or half-closed. It may be that because hamsters under natural conditions do most of their eating underground, eyesight is not important for managing their food.

Just because your hamster accepts what you offer and stuffs it into his pouches, it doesn't mean that he plans to eat it soon, or ever. He just

Below: *A gerbil (left) and a hamster may or may not tolerate each other. Two species of rodents are best kept apart.*

wants it, period. It may be something soft for bedding, or perhaps it is something that only a hamster could want.

The best diet for hamsters is a varied one, although sunflower seeds seem to be their passionate favorite. The diet should contain fresh raw greens, seeds, nuts, milk, fresh raw fruits, meats, vegetable roots and tubers, insects, eggs and prepared pelleted food. Actually, a dry

Above: *Note how this young hamster handles food.*

Below: *Dry food in cake form can be hung within reach of your hamster. Photo by Dr. Herbert R. Axelrod.*

Left: *Pelleted food is nutritionally complete and convenient to give to your hamster. Photo by Michael Gilroy.*

Above: *Two hamsters feeding on whole corn kernels and other nuts. Photo by Michael Gilroy.*

Below: *A very juicy fruit, like watermelon, is not good for a hamster. Photo by M. Gilroy.*

mixture of cracked or whole corn, kibbled dog food, dog biscuits, sunflower seeds, wheat, and peas or beans is hard to beat. Supplement it with small fresh portions of newly mowed clover or hay, vegetables such as carrot, lettuce, potato—the less highly flavored varieties seem to be favored. Given a choice, most hamsters prefer apple over orange, lettuce over cabbage. (But feed the lettuce sparingly because it is a laxative.)

Water is vital but large quantities are not required.

Soft green vegetables and fruits do not lend themselves to pouch-packing and they are often eaten on the spot. They make an excellent diet supplement for hand feeding while you are taming and training your pet.

Soft foods should be fed carefully—thoughtfully. As suggested above, the hamster's hoarding-storing system was not really made for such foods.

Most hamster owners feed their pets some sort of pelletized dried vegetable material, available at pet shops. The dried, compressed food is scientifically designed to furnish all the vital substances except water. This is suitable for your hamster's basic diet, but it should be supplemented with some treats—nuts, sunflower seeds, carrots, fruit and meat.

Sharp foods such as whole oats are also thought by some pet owners to be unsafe in the

Above: *Seeds are compressed in a variety of shapes commercially. Photo by Dr. Herbert R. Axelrod.*

cheek pouch. Fortunately, most unsafe or unwholesome foods will be rejected by your pet and that will be the end of that.

A newborn hamster is nursed by his mother until his fur grows and his eyes open. He should then get soft foods as he is weaned away from his mother's milk. Whole wheat bread soaked in milk is a fine food for baby hamsters and a fine supplemental food for their mothers. Milk sours, and so you should replace this milksop frequently.

Slightly older hamsters, and breeding females, do well if offered supplemental treats like boiled eggs, live crickets, grasshoppers, lean meat, wheat germ, and mixed birdseed (containing millet and rape seed.)

You need not be afraid of offering too much of any food to these pets. Since hamsters will not overeat, you cannot possibly overfeed them. What they do not eat they will hide away. All you must remember is to avoid feeding an excess of food which spoils or smells when it gets old.

Below: *Carrot is a good source of vitamin A. It also stays fresh much longer than most vegetables. Photo by Michael Gilroy.*

Above: *Be sure the fruit you give is fresh, not rotten or moldy, which can upset a hamster's digestion.*

If you have just one or two animals, your best source of food supply is your pet dealer who has packaged mixtures designed for hamsters. All you need to add is a watering bottle and occasional soft fresh treats like crickets, carrot, apple or a little lettuce. A *little* lettuce.

Of course, if you go in for large scale breeding it will be much cheaper to prepare your own mixes from scratch.

Some specific foods you might include in your hamster's diet are: beets, beet tops, bird seed, sunflower seeds, boiled eggs, carrots and carrot tops, live crickets, grasshoppers, corn, corn bread and cracked corn, dog biscuits, milk, lean meat, nuts, oats, potatoes and wheat germ.

All vegetables and fruits should be fresh, raw and washed. Milk should be pasteurized, condensed or evaporated. Citrus fruits are a controversial item of diet; you might try feeding a bit to your hamster and see how he reacts. (Vitamin C is apparently not required in the hamster's diet.) Cooked meats have also been a controversial food for hamsters, with some authorities believing that it induces cannibalism of young by their mothers. Others, however, disagree. Hamsters sometimes like boiled beef bones to grind their teeth on, and they probably derive

Below: *A listing of the nutritional value of the contents is usually indicated in a good commercial hamster packaged mix. Photo by Dr. Herbert R. Axelrod.*

some value from the minerals in the bone. Dry pellets and dog biscuits, incidentally, are also considered a good tooth-grinding medium.

Wheat germ oil, or substances containing it, is a good addition to the hamster's diet. Some pet shops sell ripe whole wheat as it comes from the stalk. This is as good a way as any to assure your pet of Vitamin E. Raw peanuts are also a good source of this vitamin.

Water, of course, is needed by the hamster. Much of it is obtained from the soft foods, but if pellets form a major part of your hamster's diet, a plentiful supply of fresh, clean water is an absolute must. If your watering system is working reliably, you may leave your animals unattended for a weekend with little risk. Hedge your bet with a piece of raw potato or apple for extra moisture and be sure there is a plentiful supply of grain and dog biscuits in the cage. Incidentally, many experienced animal keepers supplement the diets of virtually all domestic and

Below: *Water in an open dish can easily be upset. Photo by Burkhard Kahl.*

captive mammals with dried dog rations. This can be in biscuit or kibble form. The advantages of dry food are that trace elements are guaranteed available and spoilage is hardly ever a problem.

If, instead, you leave water in a dish in the cage, your hamster may decide that it is just the place to hoard his food or leave his droppings. In either case the result is messy.

Above: *The juice of most berries can stain the fur. You may have to wash it later. Photo by Michael Gilroy.*

Right: *A hamster will learn how to lick water from a water bottle with a drip tube. Photo by Dr. Herbert R. Axelrod.*

HOARDING

Your hamster wants to hoard his food. A female with young is especially active in this hoarding business. A nervous hamster, or one who has been recently moved, or one whose cage has just been cleaned, will stuff his pouches until they look like they will burst.

An adult hamster will keep the hoard in one place in his cage and will try to keep it as far as possible from the spot where he leaves his droppings. Try not to disturb the hoard when you clean the one soiled area in the cage.

Do not change the litter or dispose of the hoarded food more often than once a week, and preferably less often. This is especially important in the case of a female with young. Your sense of smell, at any rate, will be the best guide to how often you have to clean the cage thoroughly. You will find that a hamster cage (or even a hamster colony with thousands of cages) is practically odorless.

After your hamster has fully packed his pouches and carried his prize home he will often use his forepaws to help push the pouches from behind to unload the cargo.

Below: *Photographed at this angle, the cheek pouch of this hamster is visibly full. Photo by Michael Gilroy.*

Above: *A mother hamster may hoard food anywhere in the cage hidden from view. Photo by Michael Gilroy.*

Below: *A very strong sense of smell can lead the pups to hoarded food. Photo by Michael Gilroy.*

If you plan to breed hamsters, you will have an exciting experience. One of the great joys of pet-keeping is having your pets reproduce and watching the young grow to maturity.

Hamsters are noted for their remarkable rate of reproduction. Their period of gestation, sixteen days, is the shortest of any known mammal. The female is in season and receptive to breeding every four days. Litters range from two to fifteen, with eight the usual number of hamster cubs born. Their development is very rapid, and maturity is reached in less than three months. It's even possible to breed a hamster cub one month old although this is not recommended. Weaning is generally at about five weeks, and three to seven days after weaning the female can be bred again. Thus you can see that hamster production can be exceedingly great.

Don't try to remake hamster habits, but rather, adapt your techniques and equipment to suit what they do naturally. Hamsters are tunnel dwellers, they mate in the dark and are born in the dark and develop for several weeks in a dark nest at the end of a winding burrow, possibly eight feet long.

Most surface activity is probably at night. This is when they meet and mate. Since the nest at the end of the burrow is the nursery, the place of safety and food storage, it is defended against all comers. The female in her nest might well kill a visiting male. So, when you mate your animals, place the *female* in the cage of the *male.* The chances of a successful mating without bloodshed are increased.

For breeding purposes you should start with four- to six-

Below: *Two fancy hamsters in a mating position. Be sure to breed only healthy and mature individuals. Photo by Michael Gilroy.*

months-old stock. Provide the female with a cage containing a nest box and soft, clean nesting material. The nest box can be a compartment in a secluded part of the cage. It need not be much larger than a cigar box (no top is needed). Washed rags, tissue paper and pine wood shavings are all good nesting materials.

You can tell the females are receptive to mating when they are more active than usual. This happens every fourth day, or more properly, every fourth or fifth night. A waxy plug develops in the opening of the vagina and it is discharged at the end of each cycle. The female is receptive to breeding at the beginning of a cycle, that is to say, when there is no discharge. This examination technique may be of value to scientists working on special problems, but for breeders of pet hamsters, it is not recommended simply because there is an easier method.

Above: *An albino mother with her 14-day-old litter. Photo by Michael Gilroy.*

Below: *A cinnamon banded female with her 10-day-old litter. Photo by Michael Gilroy.*

Sometime after seven p.m. and before eleven p.m., place an active female in the cage of a large experienced male. Within a minute he will have sniffed and begun to mate with her if she is receptive. She will raise her tail and arch her back and stand still. Within thirty minutes they will be done.

Don't leave them together overnight. She will not produce a bigger litter, but she may exhaust or hurt her mate before morning.

They might not hit it off the first time. She may scuffle with him a little; this too is normal even for a receptive female, but if a fight develops, separate them immediately. Then, twenty-four hours later, try again. With this method one male can serve as many as ten breeding females with no strain on him. Remember these simple basic procedures:

Use an experienced male for an inexperienced female.

Try a female for a few minutes and remove her promptly if she is not receptive.

Repeat the routine every night at the same time until she is receptive.

Keep trying the male only until you find a receptive female, then let them mate for thirty minutes.

Once a female begins to mate, clean her cage during those thirty minutes. Fill it

Below: *A cream black-eyed mother and her brood of young creams, also all with black eyes. Photo by Brian Seed.*

Above: *Without knowledge of the pedigree of the parents, it is not possible to predict the kind of offspring which will result from a particular mating. Photo by Percy Parslow.*

Right: *These hamsters will be predominantly black later. Photo by Michael Gilroy.*

with extra bedding and extra food and plan for a litter in two weeks.

Leave her strictly alone for nineteen days and nights. If she does not deliver, try the mating technique all over again.

No matter how young your female is, somebody has probably bred one even younger. This is a meaningless exercise in diminishing returns. A female should be fully grown if you are to get any kind of production out of her. Litters from very young females are frequently born dead. If they are too small or too weak they are often killed. This may seem appalling but there is no human-like viciousness involved. Afterwards, the female hamster under *normal* conditions eats her dead or dying young as a sanitary measure.

Plan to breed a female only when she is at least eight or ten weeks old. She will probably be even better if she were twelve weeks old. Try to use an older, experienced male, the first time, anyway.

Keep records. Discard breeders which consistently produce malformed young. Leave pregnant females and females with young strictly alone. Pick up your animals in a box, can, jar or scoop. Don't handle them when transferring animals to cages for mating—your odor may confuse the issue. Avoid picking up the young, especially before their eyes open. If you must pick them up, rub a handful of grain over your hands first. It will tend to mask your odor. The babies photographed for this book were handled without loss, but the females were experienced mothers and the hand-rubbing technique was used.

The young are born blind, naked, helpless. They are about one inch long and weigh $1/4$ to $1/8$ of an ounce. After about ten days the

young begin to move about the cage and nibble soft foods, although they still cannot see. Their eyes open when they are about sixteen days old.

Litters of normal, shorthaired hamsters will range to twelve with an average of six. Stillbirths, runts and deformities might account for 2%. If your animals have a defect rate of 10%, you ought to find out why. Longhaired hamsters are somewhat harder to produce than normal shorthaired strains. Litters are small and less frequent. Possibly their long hair interferes with mating.

Most female hamsters will produce about six or seven successful litters averaging six or seven cubs per litter in a lifetime. It doesn't seem to matter if you start at age twelve weeks or at twenty weeks for the first litter; a female fizzles out after forty or fifty offspring. If you have a strain which does better, keep them and concentrate on this genetic feature.

Above: *A dove female and a long-haired lilac female. These hamster varieties are not often seen in pet shops. Photo by Michael Gilroy.*

PAIR BREEDING

Pair breeding occurs when you simply put a pair together and keep them in the same cage until the female appears pregnant. This technique usually results in a badly abused male. The female will steal his food, scratch and bite him, evict him from his sleeping area, and in extreme cases she may seriously injure or kill him.

In test or pair breeding, if a virgin female receives a preferably experienced male but does not become pregnant, do not give up trying to breed her until a second trial is made. Some virgin hamsters do not become pregnant with the first mating.

COLONY BREEDING

Some commercial breeders use a technique called colony breeding. A large cage is set up with plenty of nesting material, several water bottles, and possibly a few small nest boxes as hiding places. Three full-grown mature males are introduced to the cage. After they become thoroughly accustomed to it—after a day or so—about a half-dozen females are placed in the cage with them. Unless there are really serious fights, the animals are confined together until the females swell up or until ten or eleven days have passed. They should all be separated by the twelfth day. Don't add any new females

Below: *A young rust female and another variety called dominant spot that was developed from the piebald hamster. Photo by Michael Gilroy.*

until all those in the cage are removed. Then the three males rest a week and another six females are introduced.

The males *must* be permitted to rest at least a week between batches of females, and each female must be placed in a separate cage to bear her young.

Whatever breeding method you use, be sure the female is in her "maternity cage" at least four days before the babies are due. Don't move her until at least three weeks after they are born, and it's better if you wait four or five and the babies are weaned and go their separate ways. Then wait another few weeks before breeding the female again.

Remember that about the time the hamster is weaned, it is sexually mature, and although it is capable of breeding it should not be bred until it is four to six months old. Therefore the sexes should be separated early, before their thirty-fifth day at the longest. They will then weigh about thirty grams (approximately one ounce). A young female, to properly deliver and nurse all her first litter, should weigh at least 100 grams (3⅓ ounces) before she is bred. A fully mature, healthy breeder must weigh 150 to 158 grams (5¼

Below: *A dark gray satin male along with another male, a longhaired lilac. Photo by Michael Gilroy.*

Above: *The tortoise shell coat marking is now bred in many colors, different lengths and textures of coat hairs. Photo by Michael Gilroy.*

Right: *A female in the act of moving her new born to a different area of the cage which she considers safer, possibly cleaner and drier. Photo by Michael Gilroy.*

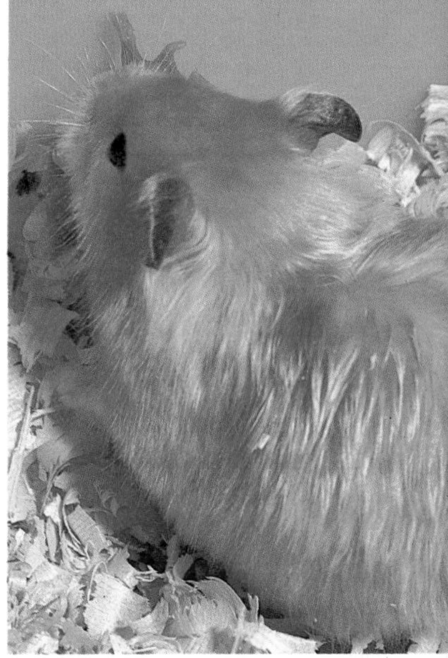

ounces). If you want to be scientific in your breeding work, you should have an accurate scale or balance graduated in quarter-ounces up to eight ounces, or in grams to about 200 grams. Some small postage scales do nicely.

COLOR VARIETIES

The hamster's normal golden color is subject to some slight variation from animal to animal. Some strains tend to be yellower, others darker. Bellies are sometimes white, gray, yellow-white or blue-white. These differences are slight and are of little interest to the casual hamster keeper. However, the serious breeder can intensify a color trait and eventually create a color which varies enough to be distinctive.

Left: *An albino angora hamster is a popular strain of hamster. However, albinos may also have undesirable and harmful traits. Photo by Burkhard Kahl.*

Above: *A black hamster. However, note the light areas around the eyes, snout and feet. Photo by Michael Gilroy.*

In addition to these slig differences, there are seve different, stand-out color strains. The albino hamste has white fur and pink eye The trait is recessive. Only pair of albinos can produce a 100 per cent albino offsprin However, two golden hamsters can produce an albino by the very rare process of mutation. This is the result of a violent gen change and each time it occurs a new strain of albino could be established. This has already happened several times. Albino offspring can also result from the mating of

golden parents if, by a rare coincidence, both parents have recessive albino genes.

Another color variation is the "pied," "harlequin," or "panda" hamster. This too is the result of genetic mutation. The markings are variable, with each strain different from other strains, and even individual hamsters vary in coloring from their nestmates. Some are gray-gold mottled on white; others are gold on white, and still other color combinations have been seen.

Pandas tend to be high strung and if you are a beginning hobbyist, you should not choose them as your first pair to breed, since they require more care than the others.

Above: *A typical piebald coat pattern of a golden hamster. Photo by Brian Seed.*

Each color variety—golden, albino, panda—can be bred to each other. The results will not be hybrids, but merely mixed strains. These mixed strains might bring more vigor to a panda or albino line, but to re-establish the recessive color trait, selective inbreeding must be done.

When breeding hamsters, aim for rich, dense fur; broad, round bodies; bold eyes; erect, uncreased ears; straight backs, and good dispositions. If you are careful about diet, care, and choice of breeding stock, your results should be very satisfactory.

Above: *The dominant spot pattern is a variant developed from the piebald. Photo by Brian Seed.*

Below: *In a hamster with mosaic pattern the spots are limited to specific areas of the body. Photo by Brian Seed.*

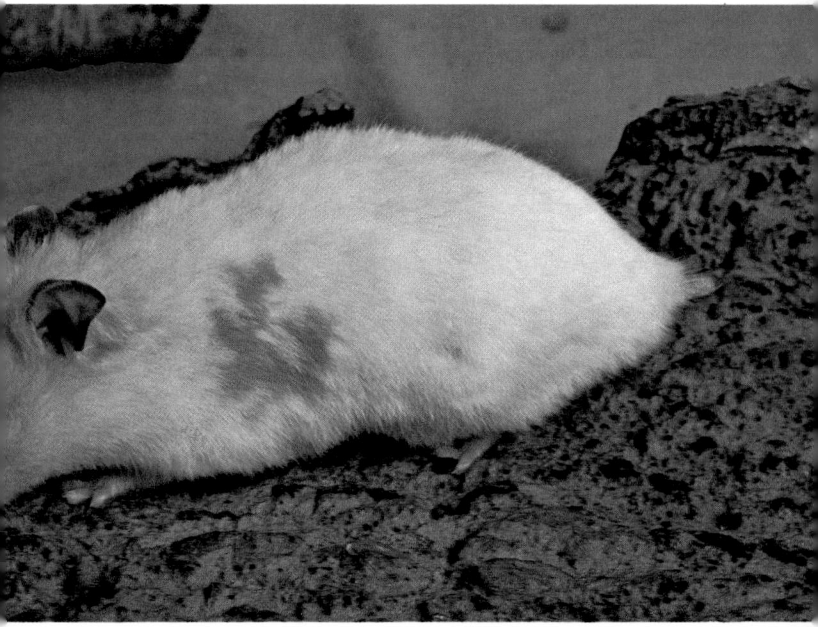

Raising Young Hamsters

Hamsters have raised hamsters for centuries with no help from us. If we insist on helping, we must do it passively. Provide the female with plenty of bedding, privacy and ample food for hoarding and eating. The water supply must be available to the babies even when their eyes are barely open. Many young hamsters die of thirst when they are weaned because the water bottle tube is so high they cannot reach it.

Soft foods, bread and milk, lettuce, meat, hard-boiled eggs are all good for babies—they will eat soft, moist bread three or four days before their eyes are fully open. They will even pack their tiny cheek pouches while their eyes are not open.

Don't help the mother gather her new litter as they are born. She will do it by herself after the last cub arrives. Keep the cage cool, dry, out of drafts, free from spoiling food, and protected from vermin, dogs, cats and little children. Keep the cage out of direct sunlight.

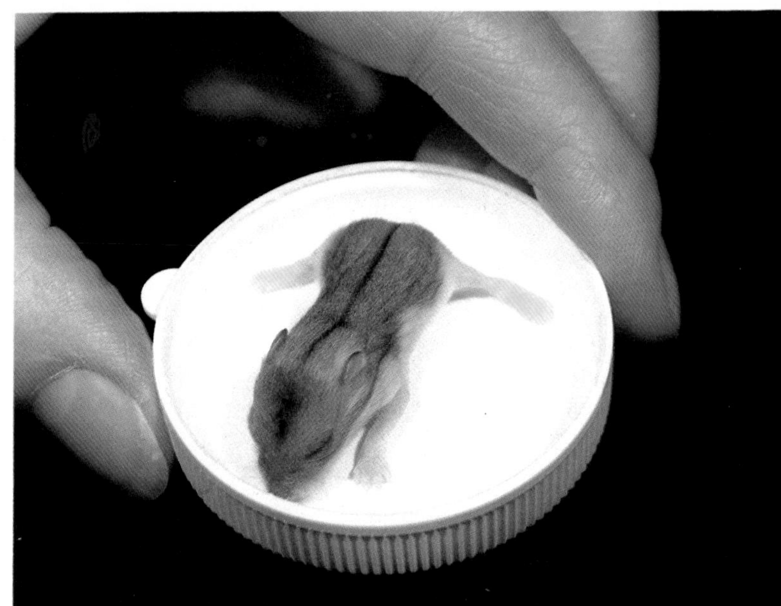

The babies should be sexed and separated after they stop nursing so that they cannot breed while too young. They might try when only four weeks old, but here is the time when you should make your presence felt.

If the mother kills her babies, it may be because you made her nervous or did not adequately shield her from some other irritant. If the mother eats her babies, it may be because she and they are undernourished, *i.e.,* underfed. If she kills them but does not eat them, it may be because she is poorly nourished, *i.e.,* lacking a mineral or a vitamin.

Left: *Appearance of newly born hamsters, just 30 minutes old. Like most mammals they are born naked and with their eyes closed. Photo by Michael Gilroy.*

Above: *The characteristic stripe on the back is already very well developed in this very young dwarf hamster whose eyes are still shut. Photo by Michael Gilroy.*

Young females who fail with their first litter often mature to become steady heavy producers of high quality young. The best productivity seems to come from females in the third through tenth months.

Hamsters are expected to live only 1000 days, and with a four day rhythm for ovulation and a two week period of gestation, the hamster has a short, intense life. If you want production, you must utilize their time efficiently. Don't let them waste it in hibernation, estivation or malnutrition.

When you raise young hamsters, give them room to grow, fresh food—including

Above: *The main activities of very young hamsters are eating and sleeping. Abnormal individuals may refuse to eat and die.*

greens and animal protein—convenient clean water and cool dry bedding. The emphasis on cool is because an overly warm hamster will estivate—go into a deep, sleep-like hibernation which is so deep you might well assume your animal is dead and dispose of him. This estivation is nature's way of carrying a furry animal over a hot period in a dry desert environment. How hot? Over 80F. is estivating temperature. Nights are cool, the hamster needs fur for his evening outdoor activity, but the hot, dry midday or hot, dry season with no rain and no juicy fruits for liquid, will induce estivation. To get your animal out of this state, circulate cool air and reduce the light.

When you raise hamsters in cool or cold places,they may hibernate. Same idea. To bring back activity, raise the temperature above 50F. but below 70F., and increase the amount of light, especially sunlight, if possible.

As you raise your hamsters, you may want to keep track of their growth. Use a 500 gram capacity beam balance and a scoop or small cardboard box to load the animal onto the balance. If the scoop has a round-number weight, say 50 or 100 grams, subtraction will be easier. A full-grown normal golden short-haired hamster will weigh about 150 grams. One outstanding feature of the longhaired hamster is his size—that is, *apparent* size, because of all that hair.

Above: *A litter of dwarf hamsters. Photo by Michael Gilroy.*

Below: *Dwarf hamsters also store food in cheek pouches. Photo by M. Gilroy.*

Hamster Diseases

Hamsters live about 1000 days, and with proper care they should never be sick. If your hamster does become sick, treat him with simple, intelligent care.

Let's start out with a few basics and then get into the details. Basic number one is that hamsters are naturally hardy and naturally resistant to disease. Basic number two is that they are subject to the same *sort* of ailments that man is subject to, and for the same reasons. That is: injuries, nutritional diseases, infectious diseases. Basic number three is that hamsters respond to disease cures much as people do. In other words, some hamsters recover with care, some recover spontaneously, and others die regardless, just like people. So much for the basics.

Detail number one is that the homily *"Cleanliness is next to Godliness"* is true. Many diseases can be cured or prevented by using clean bedding and changing it before it becomes an invitation to vermin. Remember to disinfect the cage when you change the bedding. This is easy with glass or metal or plastic cages, but much more difficult with wood. Water bottles should also be kept clean and, of course, your pet should never be expected to drink water which you wouldn't drink.

The second detail is another homily, *"You are what you eat."* Your pets should never get any more soft foods than they will *eat* immediately. *Eat*, not store. Remember the cheek pouches and the hoarding instinct. Soft foods include meat, fruits, vegetables, cooked foods and milk products—everything except grains, kibbled foods, pellets and water. Your pets should have a surplus of hard grains to hoard. This is important for their mental health as well as their physical health. Remember, they forage during the cool night and probably eat from the hoard three cool feet underground during the heat of the day. Nutrition is simple if you let your pet decide. Start with the list in the chapter on feeding and supplement it with small portions of whatever treats your pet enjoys.

The third detail concerns injuries. *Prevent* them. Treat your pet with loving, thoughtful kindness. Don't try to remake him. Don't push him to "higher" things. He is not an acrobat or flier, or even much of a climber. Cage him and handle him with the view in mind that he must never fall. Also cage him so that he cannot escape and so no cat or dog or undisciplined child can get in to abuse him. Really, that's about all that there is.

Now for cures. Let's start

Right: *An active disposition is a good sign of a healthy hamster. Photo by Michael Gilroy.*

with symptoms and then go into diagnoses and treatment.

Ruffled coat, loss of appetite, wasting, diarrhea, eventual death—this could be *salmonellosis,* an intestinal infection which can become epidemic. It may be transmitted by wild rodents or dirty drinking water or spoiled soft foods. Control and cure require that you destroy all sick animals.

No, it's not being cruel. You're saving the infected hamster from an otherwise lingering, miserable death and you're protecting the other hamsters from contracting the disease.

Isolate the healthy animals, sterilize cages and equipment. Start anew with fresh bedding and a new food supply.

As an isolated disorder, diarrhea is often the result of an overfeeding of soft vegetables and fruits—especially lettuce, as mentioned earlier—or spoiled foods.

Ruffled coat, loss of appetite, rapid breathing, nasal discharge, coughing, sneezing, catarrh. This is an inflammation of the lungs—*pneumonia.* Again, as in salmonellosis, the same measures are suggested. Also, avoid sneezing at your pets; they may catch your cold. These respiratory diseases generally occur in malnourished colonies of damp and/or overcrowded animals.

The symptoms of a *cold* are inactivity and ears held against the head. The hamster's nose may appear swollen because he ruffles his fur when wiping the nasal discharge. In advanced stages he will sniffle and sneeze, get thin, and his fur will lose its luster. As above, treat cold and sniffles with plenty of fresh, wholesome foods, a clean cage, and warm, dry bedding.

Poor general condition, loss of hair, he shakes his head and scratches his ears. Eventually, ears, nose and genitals are covered with gray warty scabs. The diagnosis is mange, caused by parasitic mites. The control is a high standard of hygiene. Wash your hands after handling each animal. Sterilize all cages and appliances. Replace all bedding. Avoid contact between infected and uninfected animals. There are mange cures available through your veterinarian. He can diagnose mange and possibly he will suggest a bath with benzyl benzoate, dimethyl-thianthrene or gammexane preparations.

Vermin and skin disorders are generally associated with dirty cages. Golden hamsters are desert animals—they don't bathe or swim by choice. But they do keep themselves clean, spending about 20 per cent of their

Right: *A healthy hamster will have a good-looking coat, shiny and smooth. Photo by Michael Gilroy.*

waking hours licking and grooming themselves. They prefer dry quarters and dry fur, and if their cages are clean and dry, with a good supply of nesting litter of shavings, straw, or other dust-free material, they will stay clean and vermin-free.

There is a fly, much like a housefly, which may deposit its eggs on nursing mothers or baby hamsters. The maggots dig into the hamster's flesh.
If there are such flies in your area, you should use fine screen on the hamster cage and remove any maggots you find. Fortunately, this species of fly is rare.

Skin parasites are not common on pet hamsters, but if they do infest your colony, you have a problem. Fleas, lice, ticks and mites are sometimes passed on from other mammals. But these pests are controllable by medications in spray or powder form.

If the symptoms are poor general condition, diarrhea, and wet and dirty hind quarters, your pet has an infection called "wet tail." This is often fatal and can become epidemic. Wet tail is often a disease of neglect. Damp cages, spoiled food and malnourished animals are generally involved. The cure is

Below: *Allow your pet to move freely out of the cage occasionally, provided hiding places are not present. Retrieving him later may prove difficult. Photo by Burkhard Kahl.*

doubtful—the control is obvious.

Constipation is another common ailment. Constipation in young or adult hamsters is directly related to the amount of pellets and water they have been fed. If you give your hamster pellets, you must provide plenty of fresh water. If you have more than one hamster, make sure that one bossy animal does not take all the water. In case constipation does occur, give youngsters milksop and greens; give adults carrots, leafy vegetables and fruit.

Running eyes sometimes indicate trouble in the cheek pouches, which may be stuffed with such food as

Above: *The female grooms her young regularly, which helps stimulate body processes. Photo by Michael Gilroy.*

bread or rolled oats that gets stuck back near the shoulder. Tears then form in the eye on the side where the stuck particle is. If this happens, flush out the pouch with water of the hamster's body temperature, using a syringe. Try to get your pet to *eat* soft foods when they are given, instead of stuffing his pouches with them.

Overgrown teeth should be snipped down with a nail clipper, and your hamster should have a bone to gnaw on.

Above: *Unless needed, refrain from handling a pregnant hamster. Photo by Michael Gilroy.*

Overgrown nails may be hereditary. Clip them, but not down to the blood vessel. If you plan to breed hamsters, don't mate any that have overgrown nails.

One form of *paralysis* may result from lack of Vitamin D. Feed wheat germ and wheat germ oil. Other forms of paralysis are the result of lack of exercise. Keep your pet in a roomy cage, with an exercise wheel or some other amusement that will provide activity. Slight paralysis can be cured by such exercise and more fresh foods added to the hamster's diet. There is not much you can do if your pet develops heavy paralysis, so it is wisest to provide the big cage and wheel to prevent it.

Infertility is sometimes caused by cold or not enough Vitamin E in the diet. Hamsters that are constantly annoyed, and hamsters that are too fat, may also be infertile. In some recently developed new color strains of hamsters, infertility may be a hereditary weakness.

Stillbirth or death at birth is often the result of falls or rough handling of the mother. Injuries which have gone unnoticed often make normal delivery impossible.

If your hamster has a *tumor, internal bleeding or skin lesions,* the best thing to do is have the vet put him to sleep.

THE OLD HAMSTER

The hamster leads a short but intense life. Any hamster that lives more than 1000 days or about two years and nine months is a rather exceptional specimen. A three-year-old hamster is a rarity.

If your pet suffers from any incurable disease in his old age, you should bring him to your vet for a painless death. You can be sure that the Nembutal, ether or chloroform used will be painless to the animal, and it is far more humane than letting him suffer.

Below: *A group of cream hamsters that are in the prime of growth. These are all females. Photo by Michael Gilroy.*

Genetics

This chapter was written by Dr. C. William Nixon of Randolph, Mass. Dr. Nixon has authored more than twenty scientific papers dealing with the genetics of the golden hamster. He has also published extensively on dog and plant genetics.

The so-called wild-type golden hamster is the "standard" from which the several variations deviate.

The wild-type Syrian hamster has short hair of the color known as "agouti." This type of coloration, which incidentally is also characteristic of many wild animals, is practically indescribable since it varies in shading according to many factors such as lighting, stage of growth, etc. The reason for this fluctuation of color is due to the peculiarity of agouti hair which is that each hair is banded by several different colors from root to apex. If you part the fur of an agouti hamster, for instance, by blowing into it, you can easily see that the base of the hairs is of a dark blue-black color. The middle portion of the hair is brownish or golden which gives the animal the general golden color we see. The pointed tips of most of the hairs are black. Therefore, there are at least three distinct color bands in the agouti hamster fur. Belly fur of the agouti wild-type hamster is of a medium to light gray usually with some irregular white patches.

Over the years in captivity, since 1930, quite a few mutations from normal or wild-type fur have occurred, and these have been perpetuated in most cases as separate lines by scientists (if the mutation had some scientific value), or by the pet trade (if the mutation was of some value to that industry in creating an attractive new type). The types of changes which may affect fur fall into three categories: (1) changes which affect overall hair color; (2) changes which affect the color pattern; (3) changes which affect the quality of the hair, that is, long vs. short.

In many respects, it is unfortunate that the term "teddy bear" was used by some breeders as the name for the variant produced by this third type of change. For example, who knows whether or not the longhaired hamster is at present or always will be the one which most nearly resembles a teddy bear? I can think of at least one other candidate for this similarity—a rare but closely-related species to the golden hamster, that in my opinion is far more teddy bear-like than the longhaired hamster. The term "longhaired" is a preferable one in that it is consistent with the same type of change in hair type that has occurred in other furred animals.

Another term in general

Right: *Longhaired hamsters are available in any color desired today. Photo by Burkhard Kahl.*

usage for long hair type is "Angora." Thus we have longhaired dogs, cats, and rabbits, the latter two of which are also known as Angora. And now, of course, we have the longhaired hamster.

There are several other known hair type mutations in the hamster which may be of passing interest to the reader, and all of them have counterparts in other animals. There are rex coated hamsters where the hair is kinky, and there are rex cats and rabbits; there are satin coated hamsters as well as satin rabbits; and finally, there are hairless hamsters in addition to hairless cats, dogs, rats, mice, etc. Overall, however, mutations for coat type are fewer in number than are those for either hair color or pattern.

Most of the hair over the back of a normal coated hamster measures 10-15 mm in length, whereas that on the longhaired hamster measures 15-25 mm and may get as long as 65 mm, perhaps even longer near the rear of the animal. To be sure, there is a great deal of variation in hair length on the same hamster and also variation among longhaired hamsters. Present data from breeding these animals indicate that the gene for normal fur length in the hamster has mutated to one for long hair and furthermore that it is a simple recessive mutation.

The symbol **"l"** (for "long hair") has been given to this factor. Normal short hair is dominant and it is designated by the symbol **"L"**. Results of breeding these hamsters also indicate that there may be modifying factors that cause variations in the length of the long hair. If such modifiers are indeed present, then it would be advantageous to select those long-haired specimens having the greatest fur length for breeding.

The formulae shown below with their ratios are the *chances* of things happening. The results one may actually get in a single litter (or even

(a) long hair (**l/l**) **x** long hair (**l/l**) = 100% long hair (**l/l**, homozygous)
(b) long hair (**l/l**) **x** short hair (**L/L**, homozygous) = 100% short hair (**L/l**, heterozygous)
(c) short hair (**L/l**, heterozygous) **x** short hair (**L/l**, heterozygous) = 75% short hair (**L/L** and **L/l** mixed) and 25% long hair (**l/l**)
(d) short hair (**L/l**, heterozygous) **x** long hair (**l/l**) = 50% short hair (**L/l**, heterozygous) and 50% long hair (**l/l**)
(e) short hair (**L/l**, heterozygous) **x** short hair (**L/L**, homozygous) = 100% short hair (50% of which are homozygous, **L/L**, and 50% of which are heterozygous, **L/l**).

Above: *A normal shorthaired albino photographed for contrast beside a longhaired albino hamster. Photo by R. Hanson.*

two or three litters) may deviate considerably from those one should get in theory. The so-called "perfect ratio" (that is, when the results of breeding are the same as those of the theoretically perfect ratio) is usually approached only when several hundred offspring of a given type of cross are added together. You consider yourself lucky if you get such a ratio in a single litter.

There are many interesting combinations that can be made between long hair type and the various colors and patterns already in existence. These combinations provide sufficient challenge to satisfy the hobbyist, as well as the budding scientist in school who is searching for a research project. For those who may wish to delve into the more technical aspects of hamster color genetics, see:—C. William Nixon, John H. Beaumont, and Maureen E. Connelly: Gene Interaction of Coat Patterns and Colors in the Syrian Hamster. Journal of Heredity **61** (5):221-228; Sept.-Oct., 1970.

PATTERN FACTORS

(1) PIEBALD **(s)** is a form of recessive white spotting. It is sometimes called "pied," "harlequin," or "panda." The **s/s** animal has irregular white patches of fur scattered throughout whatever basic color the hamster may be. A white blaze on the forehead is often present and usually indicates the **s/s** combination. In addition to white spotting, the **s/s** animal is smaller and less vigorous than its non-spotted relatives, a good example of the multiple effects of a gene.

Below: *A preserved pelt of a piebald hamster showing the typical distribution of white patches. Photo by Dr. C. W. Nixon.*

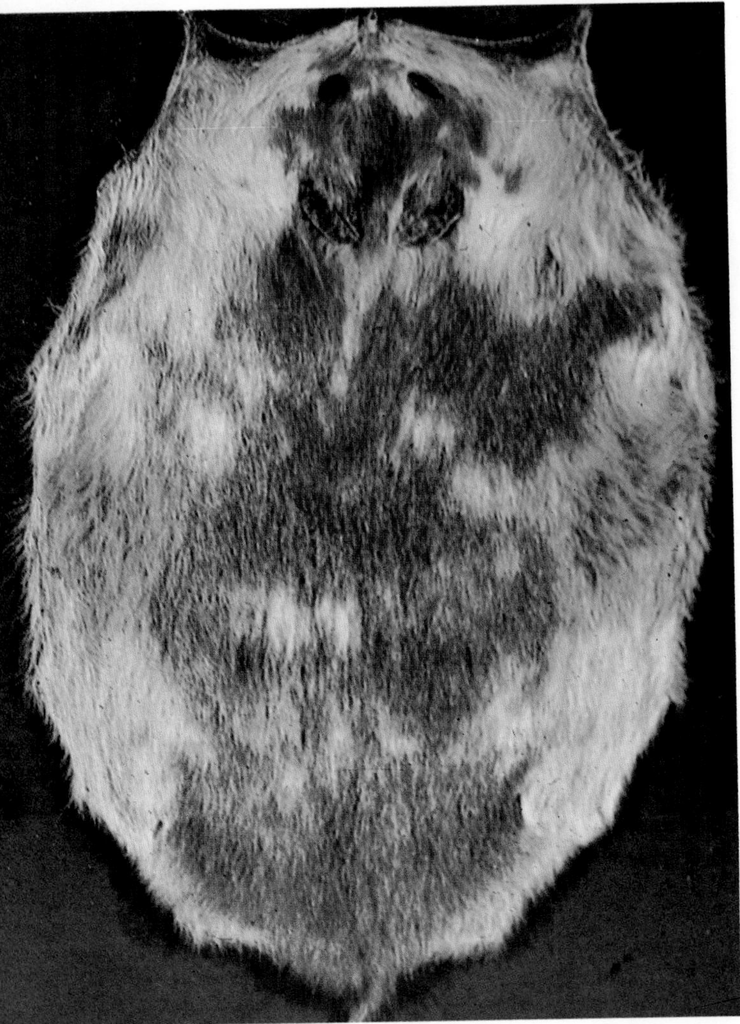

Above: *At most a dwarf hamster can grow to four inches in length, excluding the tail. Photo by Michael Gilroy.*

Below: *The coat of this hamster has been deliberately combed out to show the length of the hairs. Photo by Michael Gilroy.*

Above: *A single factor for satin is sufficient to produce the velvety texture of this satin cinnamon female. Photo by Michael Gilroy.*

(2) WHITE BAND **(Ba)**. This dominant pattern factor causes the animal to have a white band completely or almost completely encircling the trunk and thereby interrupting the basic color of the animal. Its width varies considerably and may be interrupted by a dorsal area of colored fur. White and colored areas do not intermingle, giving the animal a most striking appearance. In cases where the white band is broader than usual, it encroaches upon the shoulder and flank areas. Belly fur varies in color from almost totally gray when the band is minimal, to completely white when the band is large. The banded animal is undoubtedly one of the most attractive, especially when it is in combination with the darker colors. Since banding is a dominant factor, both heterozygous and homozygous animals have the band.

Right, top: *A banded golden hamster. Photo by Brian Seed.*

Right, bottom: *A satin golden hamster and a golden tortoiseshell in the foreground. Photo by Michael Gilroy.*

Above: *This white strain of hamster definitely has normal eyes. Photo by Michael Gilroy.*

(3) ANOPHTHALMIC WHITE **(Wh).** Homozygous **(Wh/Wh)** animals are called anophthalmic white or "blind albino." A better name for this mutant would be microphthalmic white, since the eyeballs are usually present but reduced in size in varying degrees. *"Microphthalmic"* means small eyes, whereas *"anophthalmic"* means no eyes. These animals have no pigment (white fur color and pink ears) and the eyes are reduced or appear to be absent. When present, *i.e.,* when visible, the eyeballs are pink. Rarely, homozygous animals are found that have almost normal sized eyeballs. When these apparently normal-eyed animals are bred to each other, they produce anophthalmic white young. Therefore, the parents are considered to be **Wh/Wh.** In this case, the **Wh/Wh** condition allows considerable variation in the degree of eye defects from near normal to almost total absence of eyeballs.

The heterozygous factor **(Wh/wh)** is popularly called *"imperial"* and causes the belly fur to be white instead of gray. A barely noticeable sprinkling of white guard hairs is distributed over otherwise normally pigmented dorsal portions of the animal.

Right: *Another white strain of hamster, also with normal eyes, but with angora fur.*
Photo by Michael Gilroy.

Above: Typical appearance of a young golden hamster produced in captivity. Photo by Michael Gilroy.

COLOR FACTORS

(1) ACROMELANIC ALBINISM **(cd)**. Among the color factors that have to be considered, the first is acromelanic albinism, which is a recessive factor. It is not a complete albino and should be called either by its correct name or by perhaps "black-eared white." At any rate, the fur is white, but dark pigment is present in the adult in the ears, the skin around the anus and genitalia, and the eyes which turn red with age. The weanling hamster of this type, however, may give every indication of being a complete albino, since the localized pigmented areas become so only as maturity is reached. This factor in combination with *recessive* brown **(b)** produces a pseudo-albino, thereby actually mimicking the true albino condition.

(2) CREAM OR NON-EXTENSION OF EUMELANIN **(e)**. This genetic color factor is recessive and causes the elimination of most of the dark pigment but leaves the yellowish pigment in the fur. Therefore, the dorsal fur of the **e/e** animal is one of the deeper shades of cream or yellow, and belly fur is paler yellow. The eyes are black. As the animal matures, the skin of the ears and around the anus and genitalia becomes black.

Below: A young cream angora female. Note her black eyes and dark pigmented ears. Photo by Michael Gilroy.

(3) RUST **(r)** and (4) BROWN **(b)**. These are both recessive factors, causing normal wild-type agouti coloration to become a few shades lighter, resulting in a lighter orange-brown. Belly fur is a little lighter than it is in the normal agouti animal. The dorsal fur of the brown animal is a trifle lighter in its brown to orange coloration than that of the rust hamster, but the difference is so small that it takes a skillful eye to detect it. Therefore, it is important to note that in rust animals, the eye color is black and the rim

Below: *A good representative of a rust hamster. This is a young male. Photo by Michael Gilroy.*

of the eyelid is also darkly pigmented, since these are the most obvious differences between this factor and brown. (**b**). The brown animal has dark red eyes with unpigmented eyelids. One must often rely on eye and eyelid color here in order to distinguish successfully between the two factors.

Above: *A longhaired gray hamster. Photo by Michael Gilroy.*

(5) LETHAL GRAY **(Lg)**. This is a dominant genetic factor which has another peculiarity in addition to a change in coat color from brownish-orange agouti to dark gray agouti. The lethal gray animal is always

Above: *An adult shorthaired gray hamster. Photo by Brian Seed.*

heterozygous **(Lg/lg)**, that is, it carries the normal gene. Apparently, the homozygous condition of lethal gray **(Lg/Lg)** is lethal at some early stage of development so that a living specimen is never produced. The coat is basically light gray with a silvery undercoat and a slight yellow or orange overcast. Belly fur is light gray, and eyes and ears are black.

There are several other patterns and colors known in hamsters which have not been mentioned here, but these are generally unavailable at present and can well be the topic of a complete book on hamster genetics. However, by utilizing the eight factors described here in all possible combinations, it is possible to produce several hundred different color varieties of hamsters.

How does one go about getting a longhaired hamster which also exhibits one or more of the patterns and colors? It really is not difficult, but it will ordinarily require a minimum of two hamster generations. First, you must acquire a longhaired hamster of either sex. The animal of the opposite sex should be one showing the desired color, pattern, or both. The two are then mated to produce the first generation of offspring (the F_1 generation). These youngsters will likely exhibit none of the traits you wish. The next step is to breed these F_1 animals together to produce as many F_2 young as possible, since it is here that you will get all possible combinations of factors that went into the first cross. With a little luck, you should be able to select a pair of the desired combination which, when mated to each other, should continue to produce and perpetuate that particular variety. Lethal gray ones, of course, will always produce approximately one-half of non-lethal gray offspring, even in the first

Below: *A longhaired light gray female. Photo by Michael Gilroy.*

Above: *A young golden hamster. The color and markings will intensify with age. Photo by Michael Gilroy.*

generation since it is dominant, but that poses no serious problem since it is easy to select the ones desired for breeding in each generation.

It is well to remember that the dominant factor (lethal gray, white band, and anophthalmic white) will be evident in the first generation (F_1) offspring where you will be able to select the ones for your breeding stock to produce the desired second generation. It is only at the second generation level that longhaired animals will occur in association with the colors and patterns you started with.

An alternative breeding plan would be that of breeding the F_1 animal back to its parent. This is called a back-cross and is of value only if the parents are still alive and productive. In hamsters, reproductive life begins early, proceeds rapidly, and tapers off at a rather young age. Therefore, it is conceivable that one or both parents might be beyond reproductive age (or even dead) by the time that their F_1 offspring are ready for breeding.

The conclusion of all this? The field is wide open, so get busy. It takes a little time and patience to do it, but the fun and interest generated are genuine and the price is negligible for value received. Besides, hamsters are fun. Good luck!

Genetics Glossary

Acromelanism—the color pattern where darker pigmentation appears on the extremities of the body. The Siamese cat is an example of this.

Allele—alternative characters. Long hair versus shorthair.

Back-Cross—the mating of a hybrid to one of its parents.

Dominant—a characteristic which results from either asingle or double dose of a gene. This is contrasted to a recessive which is hidden unless both genes are alike.

Eumelanin— (see *melanin*)

Gene—the unit of heredity which controls the development of a character (also called a characteristic), like long hair or pink eyes.

Genotype—the complete genetic makeup of an animal,not necessarily just what shows. Take a golden shorthaired hamster for example: Although its visible aspect (its phenotype) is golden shorthair, its genotype (its genetic makeup) may include recessive genes for long hair or white spots or ruby eyes.

Heterozygous—for a particular trait, one gene differs from its companion. See *dominant* and *recessive.*

Homozygous—both genes are alike throughout. This is the "pure" strain. There are no "hidden" recessives.

Hybrid—the offspring of parents who differ in one or more genes. Also refers to offspring from parents not of the same species. The classic example is the mule, derived from a male donkey (jackass) and a female horse (mare). Hybrids of differing species are usually sterile.

Inbreeding—mating of relatives. Brother-sister,cousins, father-daughter, etc. This will eventually result in establishing a pure breed.

Linkage—a tendency for some characteristics always to appear together on an individual. This happens when the genes for these characteristics are all on the same chromosomes.

Melanin—a complex organic compound, the pigment which is almost totally responsible for coat color. Melanin exists in two distinct forms: *(a)* eumelanin, which is varying shades of brown-black; and *(b)* phaeomelanin, which is of varying shades of yellow-red.

Mutation—a sudden genetic change.

Phenotype—the appearance of an individual; as opposed to genotype which is its genetic constitution, not necessarily apparent.

Recessive—a character which shows up only when both of a pair of genes are alike.

Variation—the differences within a species. For example, color, pattern and hair length.

Index

Page numbers in **bold** refer to photographs or illustrations.

A longhaired or angora Satin Cinnamon Hamster. Photo by Michael Gilroy.

HAMSTERS

CO-020

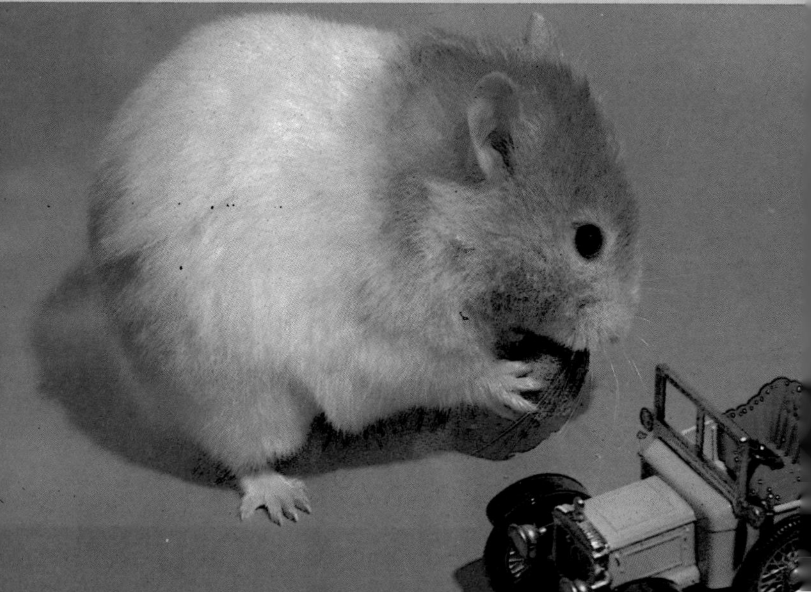

Breeders in England call this hamster variety Chocolate Banded Roan. Photo by Michael Gilroy.